A Spiritual Warrior's Path to
Re-Enlightening

Jessica Simmonds

JESSICA SIMMONDS – jessgoodvibesonly

Spiritual warrior, healer, and guide.

You need to re-enlighten every single day.
Moment by moment. Enlightenment is not a one and done.
When you become a Spiritual Warrior, I'll show you how to
light up your path.

*Please enjoy my water-colour paintings with word art
hidden throughout this book.*

66

*Only in the darkness
can you see the stars.*

– Martin Luther King JR.

This book is dedicated to me. My twin Leena. My kids Isaac, Dahlia, Charlie & Molly. My parents, Mom (Linda), Dad (Don), Darlene & Don. My siblings Terra, Ancelene & Roark. My grandparents George, Leona, John & Viney. My kid's dads Juan, Matthew & Olivier. My family & friends. For all the lessons.

"

The only Journey is the one within.

- Rainer Maria Rilke

"

INTRODUCTION

My whole life has been on purpose, for a purpose. I share these golden treasures that I have found in the hopes that you too will have a calm & clear mind and a peaceful life as a Spiritual Warrior.

Spiritual = Soul

Warrior = Brave

Guide = Shows the way to others

Re = return to a previous state

Enlightenment (enlightenment)= Self-realization and the true Self & false Self being regarded as a substantial essence being covered over by social conditioning.

You must practice re-enlightening every day to feel Love and understanding. I am a conduit for the creative energy to flow through me and I wrote this book as a transcendental writer. By becoming a Spiritual Warrior like me, you will transmute your pain into passion, power, and the gold of transformation, through subtle shifts in your reality as your mindset changes.

The next step after learning is applying. Again, remember that practice makes progress. Every single day. Repetition is a powerful way to reprogram your subconscious mind. First you learn the Truths, then you Practice.

You are creating your own reality, and I am going to re-MIND you that you are already enlightened (in the light). My peace of hope is to light up your path. We attract whatever comes into our lives. You attracted this book. It must happen first on the inside before it can happen on the outside in your projected reality. It is imperative that you become aware of your thoughts and emotions, which are energy. You must be disciplined and vigilant in ridding any negative words from your inner and outer vocabulary to create the change in your life that you've been wishing for, at every single moment. (You might feel a little "crazy" at first, being so vigilant at being positive every single moment, but it's worth it.) Just take the first step, and trust that your path will light up. You are a spiritual being, having a human experience. If you feel like you're wandering through life wondering what your real purpose is, it's because you've yet to discover a genuine connection to your superconscious mind. You hold the key. No one can save you but yourself. You simply must start where you are.

> "*Every morning, we are born again. What we do today is what matters most.*"
>
> – BUDDHA

You can sit and read books for decades like I have and get no further ahead. But the key to your success is in action. Yes, knowledge is powerful and valuable. You can fill up your toolbox and then you must use your tools. This book is an interactive guide to awakening and discovering that you are a powerful manifester. Start by choosing to walk the path of the Spiritual Warrior, to search for the truth in every moment, one day at a time.

"If you want something you have never had, you must be willing to do something you have never done."

– THOMAS JEFFERSON.

"

Unless someone like you cares a whole awful lot, nothing is going to get better. It's not.

– Dr. Seuss, "The Lorax"

"

TOP THREE REASONS TO WAKE UP

1 Everything is energy.

Once you discover what you truly are through active participation rather than just sitting and reading, you will find your power. Your thoughts and emotions are energy, so becoming aware of them is the first step on your path. Any journey begins with a single step forward.

2 Meditation and mindfulness

Power to the peaceful. Make friends with your ego. In this game of life, it's your ego's job to keep your spirit out. It has been conditioned to be your protector. You can never get rid of your ego. Your ego is designed to confuse even the most straightforward solutions, so I will simplify it.

3 You are limitless. The truth will set you free.

We are the only things in the natural world that cling; therefore, we suffer. When a leaf is ready to fall off a tree, it doesn't cling; there is no suffering. It will just let go. Until you tell yourself the truth every moment, your life will remain the same. Life cycles – you suffer when the cycle is over and are trying to continue.

Did you know?

#1 You're in earth school learning lessons, and people are your teachers

#2 There is power in words and thoughts. Positivity is crucial. Tell yourself, remember you always know how to do this. Power of Positivity.

#3 You are a powerful magnet

#4 You're creating your reality every moment

#5 The only "time" is NOW

> *There are two paths that are eternal: the path of light and the path of darkness. One path leads to liberation, the other leads to sorrow.*
>
> – THE BHAGAVAD GITA

Step one in training to become a Spiritual Warrior is to be positive for seven days straight, every moment. Swap out your negative self-talk and talk, for positive talk only. No excuses. Make this new way of being your priority.

If you are successful at this training, then continue reading this book. You will discover that anything is possible, and you are limitless.

66

If you have good thoughts, they will shine out of your face like sunbeams and you will always look lovely.

– Roald Dahl

99

TRUTHS

△

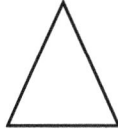

△ Get off the treadmill with your head down. Lift your head up, close your eyes to open your eye and look for the truth.

△ True Wisdom. True means in accordance with fact or reality. Wis means to know or suppose. And Dom means a state or condition. Now, having true wisdom is to know your state of consciousness which is interconnected with your level of awareness in accordance with fact or reality. That's True wisdom.

> *"In our ignorance of the truth, we have misused the highest power we possess."*
> – THE SCIENCE OF THE MIND.

△ Sugar is temporarily fixing people's low vibrating emotions. But love can get us out of here. Nothing replaces love.

△ The Truth will set you free. [You know, I've heard that saying many times in my life and never really understood what that meant. The truth comes as a feeling, not a thought. I've searched for decades desperately, trying to find the truth. I'd almost had it so many times, and then I'd fallen back asleep on my path. I'd traveled the world, lived in Mexico and Thailand every winter, escaping my reality, got married and divorced, got married and divorced again, moved over 18 times, created four incredible kids to love with three different dads, bought loads of stuff and got rid of it all, made tons of money and made no money, bought 15 different animals and gave them all away, searched for love, all the while reading and reading and searching and running away. And then boom, suddenly, just like that, I woke up for good! Finally. But there's no such thing as time, so it's only now that I'm awake. Each moment, now. It was never something that was coming in the 'future.' It's now.]

△ Words have so much power that it is called spelling because you are casting spells with your thoughts and words; remember that thoughts and words only have power when you believe them!

△ You can choose to live in joy rather than fear.

△ There really are no words to describe what you are. It's a feeling, a silence. The best way to discover this is through meditation and mindfulness. Saying you don't know how to meditate would be like saying that you don't know how to breathe. Trust your experience.

[A great way to feel this is to ask the question, what am I? Then there is a silence as the conscious mind cannot come up with an answer. That is what you are. When I started meditating on February 8th, 2020, my reality began to change. I had spent decades only reading about it all but not once did I take the time to close my eyes and go within. At first, I felt like I was crazy. Sitting there with my eyes closed looked strange to my kids as they wondered why I was napping in the middle of the day, but it didn't take long before I felt comfortable with it, and they did too. I had spent my entire life constantly on the go, and when I started meditating, I wondered how I was still alive and not exhausted to my core. The 20 min. break I'd take to meditate changed my life. I was finally meditating, and it was revealing to me finally what I really was. You can read my entire book and think "cool stuff", but until you close your own eyes, these will all just be words.]

You can live in joy now rather than live in pain

66

The truth will set you free. Light up your path; it will lead us all to the same destination. Trust that you will find the way.

– jessgoodvibesonly

99

△ You can be free of anything but yourself.

[I had traveled to 22 countries, trying to "find" myself. I was in the jungle in Mexico at a rustic retreat for hippies, writing some poetry at night when I wrote the words; No matter where you go, there you are. I was in awe of these powerful words and felt I was the only one to discover them. I then walked to the outhouse-style toilet, closed the door, and sat down to read what was written on the door in front of me; no matter where you go, there you are. It was an impressionable moment, to say the least, and it still took another decade and a half of "searching" before I got it! Waking up is here, in the now. You don't have to go anywhere to discover what you are. You don't have to go to another future time. It's only NOW. But the path can be long, and you have to keep on keeping on. Sometimes you fall asleep again for a while on the side of your path. It's time to wake up again. To re-enlighten.]

"There's a crack in everything; that's how the light gets in."

– LEONARD COHEN.

△ We are animated souls. We must remember that the universe is a multi-dimensional matrix projection of our souls, and each person you meet is a different version of you, awakening from the illusion of separation.

[If that sentence makes you trip out, you have a little more ahead on your path.]

ORDER PROCEDES CHAOS

△ Synchronicity is when you are in the flow, you'll discover that there are no coincidences, and you will be able to receive the messages from the Universe. You are being guided on your authentic path.

[I started understanding this while writing this book, I was transcendental writing like my favourite Author Henry David Thoreau. It's truly incredible! There are different ways to receive the information when you tune in to "the channel." For me, it's more like a quiet whisper of knowledge. I've always been fascinated by people who could channel, and now I can too! Yes, you can begin to do this. Our brains are all wired to be psychic.]

△ You cannot change the reflection; first, you must change the generator of the frequency, which is you.

[Loss is a result, and fear is an input. So, if you are constantly worried about having no money... Imagine you're putting a disc called NO MONEY into your player, and what's going to play is; YOU HAVE NO MONEY. If you put the disc called I AM ATTRACTING WEALTH into your player, what's now going to play is; HERE ARE SOME OPPORTUNITIES; TAKE ACTION TO GET RESULTS. There are all kinds of discs you put into your player, be aware of them. Are they negative? Because that's what you'll get back. I CAN'T FIND LOVE, etc.]

"We're all just walking each other home."

– RAM DASS

"

As a spiritual warrior, you are going to train your conscious mind.

– jessgoodvibesonly

"

"

Call all your abundance back to you. It's your birthright. The whole world belongs to you. To each person that reads these words.

– jessgoodvibesonly

"

△ It would help if you plugged back into the source. Imagine a white beam from above, coming down into and out of your body from the top of your head (crown chakra).

[Imagining this beam of white light as a visual that will help you to understand what is happening to you. I saw the most stunning art with a row of meditators with beams of white light coming into their heads and one person leaning forward with their head in their hands crying with no light connection.]

△ Creating art heals you when you discover a connectedness and joy in being a creator. Art can be anything to anyone.

[We are all artists and creators. I've been painting, writing, and creating since I was a kid, and the only difference is that I was encouraged to continue while others that stop creating may have been discouraged to follow these creative passions. There was a time when I let all of life's 'distractions' get in the way and I stopped writing and painting, but once I re-discovered the power of creating, I wanted to do it all the time!]

△ Creation is Consciousness experiencing itself, and a great scene to describe this is with Dustin Hoffman in the movie I Heart Huckabees.

[In the scene, he has a white sheet draped over his hands and punches up into the sheet to show that everything is one.]

△ Awakening is energetic upgrades, a new way of being, and integration.

[You will start to feel your energy vibrating higher. While writing this book, I got up at 5:30 every morning, excited and grateful to be gifted another day to live. I could feel and see myself changing moment by moment as I re-in-lightened more and more on every level of my being. With each lesson I learned, I'd say LEVEL UP!]

△ In this game of life, you need to remember some of these:

△ Heal generational trauma [I never understood what this was. Think of it like this. We are being raised by damaged people who were raised by damaged people that were raised by damaged people...]

△ You came to earth school with soul contracts. [You've already agreed to play roles with the people in your family and in your closest relationships.]

△ Establish healthy boundaries [This may come up with family members. You can wish them love and light but also keep your distance. With my kids, the more loving respect I gave myself, the more loving respect they gave me. When you start respecting yourself and reclaiming your power, boundaries are easy to establish without any unnecessary guilt. Boundaries are there to protect you. Set your energy boundaries, so people don't suck you into their drama realities.]

△ Teach a lesson, learn a lesson [People that come into your field of perception are teaching you a lesson, or you're teaching them one.]

△ Do shadow work [whatever bothers you about someone, a part of you wishes you could do that, or you are already doing that. For example, if they were being "selfish," I was annoyed because I wanted to be doing the same.]

△ Remember, they are holding a mirror, and they reflect your inner world [so if I found someone to be really intense, then I had to realize that I too was being intense.]

"May the path of transformation be an inspiring one as you grow more in the light".

– MARKUS ESSER

"

Figure out your patterns (dances), for real change to begin.

– jessgoodvibesonly

"

Δ If something is in your field of perception, it resonates with you. Train yourself each moment to become aware of when your cycle or lesson has started. If you know that it begins in your body as a reaction, you know you have entered a new cycle or lesson. You need to breathe and not come from a place of reactivity if you want to learn the lesson quicker. Training to control your reactions is key.

Δ Everything is based on your own perspective; remember, the same goes for everyone else. Therefore, you must "go inside" and do your own inner development. You are constantly growing and changing.

[It's so much easier to blame someone else. But remember, when you point a finger at someone, you are pointing three fingers back at yourself. Take an honest look at that moment and discover which cycle has started and which lesson needs to be learned. You will be presented with the same lesson over repeatedly until you bring awareness into that cycle and learn the lesson; only then will that very same lesson/cycle end. = LEVEL UP!]

Δ When you ask for an opinion from someone, you will take the views that resonate with your own. Also, don't give advice unless someone has asked for advice.

[Keep in mind; Never tell your 'problems' to anyone. 80% don't care, and 20% are glad you have them.]

25/75 Principle – spending 75% of your time with people who lift you up and inspire rather than bring you down.

△ With no purpose or direction in your life, you get bored. You'll then cause and attract drama into your life to play perpetrator or victim. This is a cycle that you will become aware of if you are honest and search for the truth in every moment. You will cause or attract drama into your life when you're coming from lower vibrations, conditioned body reactions, complaining, from a place of lack, judging yourself and expecting something to be coming, but remember that there is only the NOW moment and real change can happen now.

△ Are you a spiritual junkie? You are escaping temporarily with spiritual insights and mind-blowing experiences. They don't last, and you are comparing these to your moment-to-moment life, but they can't be compared to those. You can't sit and meditate, feeling you're "doing the work," and then get off your cushion and fly into a blind rage with someone. The work happens every moment during meditation and in your waking reality. But once you get to this place which is NOW and only NOW, love will come to you. You are love.

△ You must trust yourself first before you can trust another. They are merely a reflection of your own inner world. If, while in a relationship, you are worried the entire time that the person will cheat on you or leave you, then that's precisely what they are going to do! Until you trust yourself first, you cannot trust another. Loving in fear does not protect you.

When you try to live your most authentic life, some of your relationships will be put in jeopardy. Losing them is a risk worth bearing; finding a way to keep them in your life is a challenge worth taking on.

"

You are what you read/watch & Eat.

– jessgoodvibesonly

"

Δ When you're not quite far enough on your path yet and read amazing enlightenment information, it sounds fantastic, but you might as well be reading a different language.

[For me, I couldn't understand what they were saying, or it just wouldn't sink in, then I'd re-read the same thing later and get it all! I'd finally get what they were talking about. Keep moving forward.]

"What you resist, persists. What you embrace, dissolves".

– CARL JUNG

Δ Thoughts create emotions. Be aware first of your thoughts to positively influence your emotions.

[We are all chemical/energy factories. We are essentially our own pharmacies and drug addicts addicted to our own chemicals. If your baseline is low (imagine a limbo stick), you need to have 'problems,' drama and be down in the dumps to get your chemical hit. Once you raise your limbo stick higher, you can get your chemicals from joyful experiences rather than painful ones. You will feel awesome from peace, love and courage.]

66

Words have power but they come last. First there's a thought, then there's an emotion and finally the power of the word.

- jessgoodvibesonly

99

"

Stop keeping so busy.
Pause. Don't distract.

- jessgoodvibesonly

"

△ If you are being selfish, you will never wake up.

[Begin with focusing on whether you are coming from a place of lack, moment by moment. Stop and, with honesty, see where you're at. If you don't want to share something because you feel you won't get it back, get more or have something to lose, do the opposite of what your conditioned ego is telling you to do. Give a few dollars to someone on the street, buy someone a coffee without them asking, send a thank you message, say I love you, hold a door open, and whatever else you can think of daily. You will get it all back and then some!]

△ Transformation is when things change at a cellular level. Deep healing is occurring. You natural state is one of healing.

△ We are now in the age of light, and you've been training for this for lifetimes.

[When I imagined that when I re-in-lightened, my life and the world would suddenly boom! Transform! But it doesn't technically. It does transform from the inside of you, so your perception of your reality is brighter, joyful, and full of love. My living room was still full of my kids' toys, clothes, dishes & books. But it looked different in the way that I felt gratitude rather than stress. I hope this explains it a bit.]

△ You can read all the words you want for as many years as you choose, but the only thing that can truly wake you up is mindfulness and meditation. Consistent action, moment to moment. Close your eyes daily and listen to the silence in between your thoughts. You are this silence.

△ When you point your finger at someone, you're pointing three back at yourself.

[It feels easier to place the blame on someone rather than to look at yourself. Life and lessons are a two-way street.]

God means supreme reality

Δ Always remember that there is power in positivity. So keep being positive even when your spirit irritates someone else's demons.

[Become a beacon of joy. Like attracts like.]

Δ You have to give it to get it. That's what the saying should be instead of you get what you give. Could you pay it forward? Give with pure intentions to receive abundance from the Universe.

Δ You can only meet someone at the level that you have met yourself, so you need to love yourself first. You also need to get to know who you really are. Then you will meet someone that matches your energy vibration because they are at your level. Some people are worth waiting until they meet you, where you're at.

This, too, shall pass

Δ Everything is impermanent. Every moment must pass, no matter how beautiful or painful.

[If you flash back at your day while in bed, you can see nothing lasts. Not the hugs, kisses, love, or frustrations and exhaustion. Therefore, it is important to seek balance in all things and to appreciate every moment for what it is. Impermanent.]

Δ Heaven and Hell are inside of you. Not a destination that you arrive at when you die. Heaven is Joy & Hell is Fear. – Joy is the opposite of Fear, joy is Love.

Δ The three words, I love you. Heal.

Δ Love is Evol backward. Add ve, and it spells evolve. Love will help you to evolve rather than continually revolving. Love yourself and who you really are. When you evolve, you unwind, become and grow, spiraling upwards.

△ Nobody will tell you what is true and what isn't; the truth is inside you, and the information is always there; you need to remember. You hold the key to set yourself free.

Daily attention/enjoyment of life + re-enlightenment = love

△ Release resistance "It may look as if the situation is creating suffering, but ultimately this is not so, your resistance is." – Eckhart Tolle. Resistance is an inner fight against what already is. So release and free your energy.

△ Until you love and respect yourself first, you won't get love and respect back. You must also love and respect your belongings to get more.

Your body is a temple

△ You need to see beyond the deception of your ego. Daily.

△ There are different levels of enlightenment referred to by Adyashanti that happen in no particular order.

Mind (knowledge)
Heart (unconditional love)
Gut (existence and being one)

△ Awakening is a verb, and it's not a destination to arrive at. Instead, there are layers on the path until the truth is known to you. Then, you start to open up into the expansiveness of the Universe. Enlightenment is indescribable with words because it's different for each individual.

[I started to feel excited to wake up in the morning, thankful for another day here in earth school! Ready to see the beauty and learn my lessons. I had re-discovered my purpose. Your life at first won't be any different than it was on the outside, but your perception of it will change completely. Coming from a place of pure love, you will be transformed instantly.]

△ Happiness is purpose and flow. So, in the beginning, smile and fake your happiness until you make happiness your reality.

△ Any animals or insects that come to you during the day are messengers sent. See what messages they have for you.

There is no other time but NOW

△ You are a Devine being, and you can run at full power. However, you have been holding back. Access source energy to heal from within, and remember that you are transparent.

△ The word understanding broken down says under standing. You need to be grounded to channel and receive the information. You can think of your superconscious (the pineal gland) as a way to receive messages from your angels, guides, and higher self.

△ To level up, you will be required to push yourself past who you currently know yourself to be.

△ Divine timing is real. My mom always said, "Don't push up against the universe."

△ Think of "rejection" as "redirection" instead. Sometimes it means to redirect your actions.

Δ If you know someone with dementia, they have an intense awareness of the present moment; they've transcended their personal self and are connected to the universe.

Δ Get into your body to get out of your head. Be fully present in your body.

Δ The term "in the zone" is also called "frictionless flow," a state in which you encounter no resistance to anything you do.

Δ Boomerang karma, as I like to call it. It's the law of the Universe that all actions have consequences that will affect the doer of the action at some point in the future.

"Life can only be understood backward, but it must be lived forwards."

- SOREN KIERKEGAARD

"

We are endless
dreamers, and we are
together again in
THIS dream.

- jessgoodvibesonly

"

△ When you are at your best, you are in social engagement mode. [Get out, walk around the city or town you live in, and act like a tourist. Letting new experiences and adventures happen.]

△ If you take the time to meditate and let yourself connect to the source, your body will stay healthy. If you do not take the time to do this, you will get sick so that you can reconnect through sleep and rest. (Synonyms of the source are head and original.)

△ There are layers to re-in-lightenment, like an onion. But, once you start peeling back the layers and seeing the truths, there is no going back. This is a good thing.

> *"Don't worry about what others do or don't do. Rather, pay attention to what you do or fail to do."*
>
> – THE DHAMMAPADA.

△ Ctrl-alt-delete - If you want to understand what programming means and which programs you have, an example would be if you lift your pinky finger when you drink from a glass; that would be something that was programmed into you as a child. You'll learn most of your programming from home and from whoever raised you. It's time to hit ctrl-alt-delete on most of that stuff.

[I realized how programmed I was when a friend asked me if I wanted a drink of pop, and I said; no way! I don't drink pop! And then I laughed and said yes, give me a drink! Because I realized that's how I've been programmed. He asked which cult I was in, and I told him, my own cult! My twin sister and I shoplifted with a friend when we were 15 and I still (not anymore) feel like people think I'm stealing. I think it's time to ctrl-alt-delete that programming that I made for myself. These are the things you need to look at with a magnifying glass like Sherlock or Enola Holmes.]

△ Did you ever wonder why babies sleep so much? It's because they need to connect back to the source.

△ The saying is that curiosity killed the cat, but the cat is connected to the source and is curious every moment because it lives in the now. It doesn't live in the past or the future. So that saying is meant to throw you off. Curiosity is how you re-in-lighten.

△ Just because a baby cannot speak your language does not mean they aren't speaking. Sound is vibration, and when you are awake to this channel, you will be able to hear their needs and wants as though they were talking to you.

△ When you pay attention, you get paid (rewarded).

> *"How shall I grasp it? Do not grasp it. That which remains when there is no more grasping is the self."*
>
> – PANCHADASI

△ You'll become inspired by life! Inspired means of extraordinary quality, as if arising from external creative impulse.

Take ownership and accountability for your life. Your reality. Stop looking for drama.

△ Magic potions are energy. There are elixirs and essential oil blends that can assist your energetic needs.

Hold on to the truth to let go

△ When you believe in love, then you are rewarded with love. Therefore, you need to love yourself; first, this is the most important gift you can give yourself.

△ You must step outside of your comfort zone for change to happen. It's uncomfortable, but you've got this. Your ego thinks it's been protecting you and keeping you safe in your cozy bubble.

△ The only time is NOW. Past, future, and present are all NOW.

△ We remember our life by moments.

△ The truth is love, and the source is love. The Universe doesn't want you to try harder; it wants you to trust it more.

△ Heaven or Hell and inside of you. They are not places you go to. They become your reality based on what's happening on the inside of you.

△ A new baby keeps their fists closed to hold onto their energy.

△ The seat of my soul is with bare feet on the ground sitting on my Adirondack chair in our yard, facing the sun.

> *"We must be the change we wish to see in the world."*
>
> - GANDHI.

△ Meditation is the most effective way to access your superconscious mind (you cannot roam aimlessly through life any longer without any sense of what you truly are). If you feel you have been, you're missing the connection to your superconscious mind. You will get behind your incessant thoughts and find who you are. Once this happens, you will discover the true meaning and purpose in this life. Magic follows high-vibrating emotions.

△ Every single mOMent (moment says OM in the word, it is the essence of the entire Universe and Consciousness.) is in the NOW, and it's always different and NEW.

△ You're just like a seed being blown around aimlessly by the wind, you need to plant yourself, grow your roots and rise.

Buddha translates to awakened one

△ The power of ancient plant medicine; Ashwagandha is a spiritual powerhouse along with Holy Basil, Gotu Kola, and Curcumin.

△ Your outer world changes when your inner world does. Turning your focus inwards is the only way to expect any change in your reality.

△ How you think and feel creates your STATE OF BEING. Choose the bright side.

△ We are our own pharmacies; you created it, and you can heal it.

> *"Age is a case of mind over matter; if you don't mind it, it doesn't matter!"*
>
> – MARK TWAIN.

△ We are made of energy. We are also chemical (energy) factories. You cannot connect to your light when you are constantly in flight/flight/freeze mode. You need to be in light/rest/digest mode to ascend.

[As you ascend, you start to remember more and more. This is because your mind and ego were set up to hold you into the illusion with repetitive thoughts which create emotions.]

Δ You believe in unseen forces and energy, such as the wind, the internet, viruses, germs, and your breath. So now, consider that your thoughts and feelings are just as real. They aren't just something happening in your body and mind.

[Don't get played by your thoughts and emotions. Becoming aware with non-judgment and love for yourself as you're training is the best way to move forward.]

Δ Your energy field or aura radiates 2-5 feet outside your body.

"

*Don't chase. Attract.
Stop circling and
spiral upwards into
ascension.*

- jessgoodvibesonly

"

Δ The saying is; seeing is believing, but it should be believing is seeing.

Δ It can get kind of "rough" when you dismantle reality. First, you need to dismantle your perceived identity and fears.

Δ The saying: sticks and stones may break my bones, but words will never hurt me is not true. Words are energy, so they do hurt. When you raise your awareness and vibrations, you will no longer be able to be around someone hurting you because you are no longer hurting yourself. (If you are internally hurting yourself with words, this will be reflected in the people you're around.)

Δ The way of the middle path is essential. Balance is key.

Δ You are a powerful manifester. You need to perceive your reality from your heart center. Train yourself to feel what resonates in your heart center.

Choiceless awareness

Δ You can change your brain just by thinking alone. Which other way is there to do it, right? Get started now.

Δ Every single moment, you are entirely a new being. You are NOW in a cycle that's spiraling upwards.

Δ Once you feel connected to the source, your powerful healing will begin.

Δ Remember that your past stories become your habits, which create your comfort zone and cycles. Change only happens when you step outside of your comfort zone, and it may feel uncomfortable in your body. However, small steps create confidence, and start to build from there.

△ Think of your body as the subconscious mind (feeling) and your conscious mind in your head (thinking).

> *"If you want to find the secrets of the universe, think in terms of energy, frequency, and vibration."*
>
> – NIKOLA TESLA.

△ You will meet your match when you meet yourself.

△ There is no location or time. You are creating your reality. [The sun rises and sets to give the illusion of time passing. Say, the sun stayed in the same spot in the sky all day long and through-out the night. Would it feel as though time was passing? Your imagined energy levels also drop and rise through-out your day based on your conditioning.]

Joy makes you young

66

Losing your mind is a good thing. Staying grounded helps during your controlled psychosis.

- jessgoodvibesonly

99

△ Train yourself to stop and pause before you react and do the opposite of what you usually do.

△ You need to shift your perspective to shift your consciousness.

Train your mind to focus on how to react, respond and commit to what you want in life, at your own pace and at your own time. Which is now.

LOVE STORM

△ In a world where you can be anything, be kind.

△ Chakras are spiritual energy fields that allow divine forces to flow through them. Sunlight and food are energy sources that help to charge our chakras.

△ Atonement is At-one-ment.

△ This is your earth school, and your lessons guide you towards love, purpose, and remembering what you really are. You are on the planet of emotion.

△ The best things in life happen when you feel the energy of fear and do it anyway.

△ Your brain detects your mind as the 6th sense. Just because you can't see the unseen doesn't mean it doesn't exist. Use your other senses.

The teacher will come when you are ready

△ Everything is constantly changing, moment to moment. So every moment is NEW and NOW.

△ Channeling is tuning into the information field as you would tune into a radio station.

[I'll demytify channeling by letting you know that it feels like you are tuned into a radio station with ideas! Incredible and creative ideas flow to you.]

> *"When one door of happiness closes, another opens, but often we look so long at the closed door that we do not see the one which has been opened for us."*
>
> – HELEN KELLER.

"

We are all connected
by our breath.

- jessgoodvibesonly

"

MANS
VOLVE
BE STRONG.
FLY.
REVEAL
CHANGES IN THE WIND.
GOOD
A WORLD
communicate.
wish
the light
ENERGY
life exists
JOURNEY
INSID
invisible
Interstellar dust
en route
Now
within
One step at a time...
BECOME
NIQUE
LIFE

MORNING RITUALS and DAILY RITUALS

[These are important so that you can be re-in-lighten every day. You could discover what yours are. I like to light an incense stick to symbolize my daily re-in-lightening.]

△ You have soul contracts with the closest people in your life. Some people are either your coaches, trainers, or your cheerleaders. Think of each person in your life and see what role they play so that you can learn your lessons to end the cycle and ascend.

> *"The space between your thoughts is the window to The Cosmic Mind."*
>
> – DEEPAK CHOPRA.

Everything is energy vibrating

△ You need to do your inner reflection work first, so that action on the outside comes back to you and mirrors your inner world transformations. Then, you need to make the changes on the inside by becoming aware of your cycles and lessons.

[I discovered that one of my cycles was that I would end a relationship in a tumultuous way so it could end. And I had abandonment issues like almost everyone does.]

△ Once you know your own worth, then your partner or future partner will know your worth.

△ Like a magnet, you draw people into your field of perception or awareness for a reason.

△ Depression is deep rest from playing the character you've been playing.

△ Train yourself to see the potential.

MORE SELF LOVE

△ Learning to ignore things is one of the great paths to inner peace. After that, you will be unaffected by anyone's emotions; they will pass through you.

△ It's time to level up.

△ TRUTH (left side and breathing in)

△ LIES (right side, coughing, breathing out, and sneezing)

△ Crying breathes in the truth, holds it, shakes all of your energy up to your head, and releases through your eyes and sounds from your mouth.

△ Laughing blows out the lies, and you laugh outwards. Shaking your energy and sounds out. Moving this stuck lower vibrating emotional energy up and out often is important. It will move from the lower vibrating chakras (energy centers) below the heart and up and out the upper higher vibrating chakras.

> "This fleeting world is like a star at dawn, a bubble in a stream, a flash of lightning in a summer cloud, a flickering lamp, a phantom and a dream."
> – DIAMOND SUTRA

Grounding Techniques

△ Cold water therapy and washing your face with cold water

△ Senses (food, scents, music, singing, nature)

△ Breathwork

△ Moving your body and massage

△ Earthing (free electrons/potent antioxidants) are transferred from the earth into your body

△ Meditation

△ Crystals (black obsidian, red jasper & hematite)

△ Sunshine and fresh air

Activate the vagus nerve (puts your body into light, rest & digest mode), activating your pineal gland, a.k.a. super consciousness:

△ Chanting, humming, singing, gargling, clicking tongue

△ Yawning

△ Holding breath (box breath)

△ Foot massage

△ Laughter

△ Yoga

△ Moving body (pulling in the stomach into your belly button, standing tall)

△ Meditation

△ Deep breathing

△ Cold water therapy and cold water on your face

△ Sun gazing (sunrise & sunset)

△ Moon bathing

> *People can suck you into their manifested reality (look for your truth)*

△ Putting pressure on the microcrystals in the pineal gland produces an external electromagnetic field (stretches your field out called the Taurus Field). You can access your super consciousness and pick up information on this "channel."

△ Most people don't even know themselves, what does it matter what they think of you?

△ Your body is a magnet with a north and south pole. The north is positive, and the south is negative. Most people have energy stored in their lower three chakras. Thoughts are stored as energy drawing into your invisible field around your body rather than from the infinite source. You need to pull your mind out of your body. Your breath is used to deliver energy back to your brain.

> *"Life is a game made for everyone, and love is the prize."*
>
> - AVICII

"

You must WAKE UP to what you truly are. It's like coming alive again.

- jessgoodvibesonly

"

> *"You have to keep breaking your heart until it opens".*
>
> – RUMI

△ Get living in joy and truth or keep living in suffering and lies.

△ Hear no evil, See no evil, Speak no evil.

△ It's one thing at a time, moment by moment.

△ Bigger, better, and more will never fill the void inside until you see what's on the inside.

△ Procrastination is not accepting the now and wanting to rush to the next moment.

> *Two of the best things aren't things. Love and finding out what you truly are.*

△ Happiness is a state of mind, not something to buy or find. We all share the same things in common, we laugh, and we cry. This is our wild and glorious life.

> *No matter where you go, there you are.*

△ Our body releases the same amount of chemicals to produce (fight/flight/freeze) that it would for a phone bill that's due or if a lion was chasing you. So you can't spend your entire day in that release of chemicals and not expect consequences for your energy field and body.

Laughter unites us all

△ You are in a relationship with someone because your energy vibrates at the same frequency. When they no longer match, then the relationship has expired. Since there is no such thing as time, it all comes down to vibrations and lessons. If you're asking yourself if the relationship is over. The answer is, more than likely, yes.

△ When you are in your upper chakras and not in the dense lower body chakras below the heart chakra, you can tune in to the proper channel to receive information from the Universe, your guides, etc.

You can only see clearly with your heart

"

If you only knew the magnificence of 3, 6, 9, then you would have a key to the universe.

– Nikola Tesla

"

GOLDEN KEYS

- 🔑 Faith
- 🔑 Resilience
- 🔑 Zero-expectations
- 🔑 No-judgements
- 🔑 Awareness
- 🔑 Gratitude
- 🔑 Forgiveness
- 🔑 Be kind
- 🔑 Choose positivity = happy
- 🔑 Purpose
- 🔑 Balance
- 🔑 Commitment

PRACTICES

☮

☯The next step after learning is applying. Again, remember that practice makes progress. Every single day. Repetition is a powerful way to reprogram your subconscious mind. Remember that "practice makes perfect." Practice, learn, repeat.

There are yin yangs available to check off the practices you have completed. In addition, there's a heart for you to circle if the practice resonated with you and an upside-down heart if it didn't yet.

When you learn a lesson, say to yourself:
LEVEL-UP

☯ Breath in the air and say; I am safe. I am loved. ♥ ♡

☯ Your hearts knows the way to happiness. However, your head can overthink, rationalize, and doubt almost anything. Close your eyes and ask yourself, "Am I happy?" feel the answer. ♥ ♡

◐ The Universe is inside you meditation. ♥ ⬥

Step one is discovering what you truly are. There are no words to describe this exactly. Here is a meditation that I created to assist you in seeing your power and beauty. You are a light being, and the Universe is inside of you. See for yourself.

This is a new technique that I discovered. This meditation will access your superconscious and allow you to see the light being that you are. Press your hands into your closed eyelids for a few moments to see the light. Blink your eyes closed to see new kaleidoscopic images. Light, Universe, pineal gland, third eye, circles, colors, and more. Breathe in for 4 and hold for 2 and out for 4. Release your hands and keep your eyes closed to see your third eye. Ask the question, who am I? Then you'll see there really are no words to describe the beauty of the being you are. (Practicing this first thing in the morning or before sleep is best)

◐ Follow these steps: Make new rituals. Go to a farmer's market. Look into the cars of others and see that people are all living out their own realities. We are all connected by our breath in sharing our world of realities. Don't distract, actually look at people. Leave a tip in a TIP JAR. Smile at people without expecting one in return. Be a silent observer. ♥ ⬥

You must commit to training your body like a dog, to sit and stay to meditate. Your mind will come up with many reasons why you don't have the time to do "this," like you have other things to do, it's boring, you don't get it, etc. Treat learning to meditate just as you would when learning any other sport or skill. There are several different and unique styles of meditation, but the results are all the same. Remember that there is no right or wrong way to do it.

☯ Expansive practice – look up at the vastness of the sky and say ahhh as you breathe in. Pause. Say ahhh as you breathe out. ♡ ⬥

☯ This is a freeing one you can do alone or with a friend. Start saying any random words out loud without any thought; feel and allow whatever comes out to come out. Don't try to speak your language; make up random word sounds that aren't your language that you currently speak. You will be surprised to see that you will speak another language that is a part of you. ♡ ⬥

☯ Set your screen saver and home page to inspirational words such as: Take a deep breath. You are limitless. This might be one of the most significant changes you make if you pick up your phone throughout the day. Turn off all notifications that aren't absolutely necessary and change your notification sounds. ♡ ⬥

☯ List some things that you loved doing as a child. Re-discover the positive things about your inner child. The activities that brought you joy. ♡ ⬥

[I know my favorite things to do as a child were, playing outside, going barefoot, digging in the dirt, being in the sunshine, playing in the rain, writing, reading, singing, laughing, cleaning, decorating, creating, climbing trees, collecting treasures, riding my bike and more. Most of us thought we had to "grow up" and be serious because that's what grown-ups do. Do you believe now that you shouldn't do the things you once loved? Didn't think so.]

☯ You are larger than the Universe. Sitting meditator meditation: You sit in a meditative position and imagine that you are growing into a statue bigger and bigger. (You can be any color you imagine) 🖤 🤍

[I had been meditating for almost 2 years on couches, chairs, and beds. I had yet to bring myself to sit on a meditation cushion. Then while creating this book, I bought a beautiful peach, gold, and light blue round cushion to meditate on. I felt a burning down my back as I sat there properly for the first time, but I knew that the feeling was energy coming down into my crown chakra. Connecting to the source.]

Every moment you need to remember: The Truth, your breath, and NOW

Once you've re-in-lightened, you start to go through your life like a bat with echolocation. So whatever you're putting out, positive energy, you will get positive energy back, so you know your direction.

☯ My daughter told me in her dreams, she looks up with her eyes to leave that dream and go into another dream. So anytime during your day, look up with your eyes to reset your brain. 🖤 🤍

☯ Let your rhythm change your life on this earth. Dance! Celebrate life! 🖤 🤍

☯ You have to get out and live for things to happen to you. Do new things and have experiences to build confidence like you did as a child. Don't wait to find out when you're old that THIS WAS YOUR LIFE! 🖤 🤍

Close your eyes, put your head down, and raise your hands in the air and shake them like you just don't care. ♥ ▲

Put on a finger light and visualize your power. This is also a fun activity to do with kids. Think E.T. style ♥ ▲

Ignoring doesn't work. Be honest with yourself right now. You cannot ignore the big things that happened in your past because the energy is stored in your body. You need to release it. ♥ ▲

[While writing this book, I cried harder than I had in years. I was ignoring that I cared about my second ex-husband still after 5 years (we were together for a decade) and it bothered me that we never talked anymore. I ignored that I wasn't talking to my dad and didn't speak to my first ex-husband, whom I walked out on and never talked to again....]

I never felt something more healing in my life, than when my little girl dried my tears and petted my head to make me feel better for her pain and my pain together. Since we are young, we want to not feel alone. We want to be loved and to be heard, that was all we ever needed. ♥ ▲

When someone's sick, tell them I hope you feel better.

Look deeply into some one's eyes and hold. Say I love you keeping constant eye contact. Feel the power. It makes you happy and as my daughter says when we do this, it makes your eyes shine, Mommy and it makes your teeth shine, Mommy. ♥ ▲

Stop rushing. ♥ ▲

[I saw firsthand the value of not rushing to the next moment when a woman hit a man on his bicycle while dropping my kids off at school. They both learned lessons. Life is about learning the lessons and people are your teachers.]

☯ Drink a fizzy drink of choice and belch out all of your lies. Don't think about them; just let them come out. ♥ ◐

[I visited an incredible church in Chiapas, Mexico, where there were pop bottles lined up along the interior walls. People would go there to belch out any evil spirits inside of them. Your lies are what you need to rid yourself of, so you can focus on the truth.]

☯ Practice letting things go. I've always heard the term non-attachment. I never really got it. Now, I do. ♥ ◐

[Over the summer, I lost my phone three times and was peaceful and okay with losing it each time. My kids and family thought I was crazy, but I knew it would be alright and work out. The third time I lost it, it was never found. I let the feeling go of losing pictures, notes, and phone numbers. If people are all this attached to a piece of plastic that is mainly glued to their hands, then the world has a real problem. Haha. Of course, I replaced it with a new one, but the lesson was non-attachment, and I learned it quickly. As I write this book, my driver's license is missing. I find it funny, though, because I say my old identity is gone.]

Okay, so... you input fear, and you get loss. You're a magnet, and if you fear anything, you get loss back. Love, money, friendships, life, etc. With all honesty to yourself, where have you been inputting fear?

Everything's Gonna be all-light meditation: Close your eyes, smile, and hold it. Focus on your breath and look up slightly with your eyes closed to reset. ❤ ◗

You must reclaim your power. Imagine you are a power bar with plugs going to different things. You need to access the ones that drain all your energy with absolute truth and remove them or find more balance. Is it your guilt, phone, addictions, or fears? ❤ ◗

66

"We are all creator beings."

- jessgoodvibesonly

99

☯ Bless your food or drinks with love and light before they enter your body. Their energy will vibrate higher. ◉ ◉

☯ Your distractions take you off track of finding out what you really are. So what are your excuses to not sit and meditate or escape each moment? ◉ ◉

☯ Starfish meditation: Lay on the floor with your arms and legs open in the position of a starfish. Imagine sinking into the floor or floating up. ◉ ◉

☯ Pay attention to people's perceptions of their reality and see their Drama. They think they need to have stress to get that hit of chemicals. But they can get more from positivity. Don't play into their reality to fit in. Their baseline is low (where they get the chemical release from), so they need to get down there to "feel better," but the baseline needs to be raised, so you can get your chemical release from higher vibrating emotional, chemical releases since we are all our own energetic pharmacies (and we're addicted to our own made chemicals.) ◉ ◉

[Drama happens when you're not paying attention to get your attention. My twin sister and I fought a lot in our lives. Since we both re-enlightened at the same time, we were in this together. One day, our ego's started to yell at one another, but it didn't last long. Within minutes we laughed and said to our egos; good try; we don't need drama anymore! haha]

You must be mindful of who you spend time with, what you listen to, watch, learn, etc.

☯ Peeing is one way we release our emotions. You need to drink lots of water to release your emotions. Teas and coffee are diuretics that help you to pee more. But you need a cup of water for each cup of coffee. ♥ ⚪

☯ The I LOVE YOU circle. Stand in a circle with friends, family, and kids and say over and over to one another; I LOVE YOU! ♥ ⚪

[The first time I discovered this was with two of my kids and two of my nieces. We all started saying; I LOVE YOU! It was the most beautiful connection! So much love and so many smiles.]

☯ You need to release all unnecessary things to release unnecessary thoughts. Different methods of removing stuff from your living space that you no longer need exist. The main idea is to start with categories. When you awaken, you will see that you have too many things. My great uncle had a saying; "a place for everything and everything in its place." So release your stuff to release your "stuff." ♥ ⚪

☯ Try this the next time you eat. Breathe with your nose as you chew, and you can only taste your food while breathing out. When you are chewing and breathing in, you taste nothing. Also, go to a restaurant and release inhibitions by eating messy foods like a burrito, and don't try to control how properly you're eating. Instead, take a big bite and let the food fall. No one cares as much as you thought. This practice is freeing. No one watches; if they do, they'll be embarrassed for looking and then look away. ♥ ⚪

"

YOU

ARE

WONDER

FULL

"

☯ You can only do powerful visualizations when you are in the hypnogogic state (before sleep and upon awakening.) Lay comfortably with your eyes closed and feel/visualize your happiest and authentic self and that self living the life of your dreams. The sky is the limit, as you are limitless. Everything you want is already available to access inside of you. ♥ ⬥

☯ Control your emotions and reactions every moment. ♥ ⬥

☯ Make space in your life for NEW things and people to enter. Break old cycles to allow for new cycles. ♥ ⬥

[After almost 2 years of meditating every single day, I stopped on purpose for two days to see what would happen. I felt like I was being pulled in all different directions, running around like a chicken with its head cut off. Stressed out and rushed.]

Love, consciousness, and bliss

☯ Eat off of beautiful plates and bowls and drink from fancy cups. Use magical cutlery. ♥ ⬥

☯ Let go of your "lack" to receive more money. Reset your gratitude meter. ♥ ⬥

Observe, don't absorb

◉ It requires commitment and dedication to speak positively to yourself. ♥ ◗

◉ The act of yawning puts pressure on the pineal gland sending more light into your body. ♥ ◗

◉ Find your gratitude and start thinking of everything right in your life rather than what's wrong or missing. ♥ ◗

◉ Imagine people holding up mirrors. So what bothers you about them is actually your reality. It has to happen on the inside first before your reality is created on the outside. Therefore, the saying "I know you are but what am I" is not that far from the truth. ♥ ◗

You've got to give it to get it

◉ Rest and digest breathing to activate the vagus nerve (essential for transporting light through your body and catapulting your spiritual progression). Then, say, "I am safe." The vagus nerve is rest, light, and digest. The opposite of fight/flight/freeze. ♥ ◗

◉ Are you a dust ball storm or a floating speck in the universe? Follow the flow and the path of least resistance to find the answers. ♥ ◗

◉ Before you enter a room with others, silently wish them all love and LIGHT. ♥ ◗

"

If you can change something, don't worry about it. If you cannot change something, don't worry about it.

– Dalai Lama

"

☯ Remember that *dramatized* can turn into *traumatized*. ♡ ♡

☯ Put your hands into the shape of a circle and say, "I am healed, I am whole, I am a soul, and I am home." ♡ ♡

You get what you allow

☯ Music healing. Put on your favourite sad songs, lay back on the floor with your feet up on the wall like you did as a teenager and heal/feel all of the pain. ♡ ♡

☯ Clean out every recess of your home to clean out every recess of your mind. ♡ ♡

☯ It isn't ironic that the two poses to help relieve lower back pain are happy baby and a deep squat that resembles having a baby. It is a deep-rooted pain related to your emotions. ♡ ♡

Praying hands signifies the potential for a spiritual awakening

☯ Try some channel writing or typing. Start by writing with a pen to paper or typing. Don't think. Just start writing. You could ask a question to receive the answer or simply start writing. You'll be surprised that answers and information start pouring out when you don't think about it. This information is from your higher self and is always available to you. ♡ ♡

☯ Be aware throughout the day of when people hook you into their realities (ask the truth in each moment if you want to be in their reality) ♥ ♡

☯ I surrender to the universe practice: Lay in bed on your back with your hands up over your head and say ahh (the most expansive sound) and then say; I surrender. ♥ ♡

☯ When you find your thoughts or emotions to be negative, simply and diligently replace them with positive ones. Each moment. Diligence, when combined with faith, assures spiritual success. (The word diligently means gently. Go easy on yourself, no judgment.) ♥ ♡

You can meditate easily. Neuroscience &
quantum physics bring you understanding.

☯ You've got to admit what you already know. Find out what your patterns (dances) have been until this point in your life. What are your broken records or repeated cycles? Awareness is the key. ♥ ♡

[When you discover your dances, you wake up more and more. That's why reflecting on your past "lessons" is key. I found my love relationship dances when I started to wake up in my heart more and more. My dad always told my twin sister and me to take our ugly pills as kids to make us ugly since he said we were getting too beautiful. He said this as a loving dad in the best way possible. We were also taught never to look at our reflections too long in public so we wouldn't look "full of ourselves." Every man I was in a relationship with never told me that I was beautiful, but I never told myself that, and if they were reflections of my inner world, how could they tell me that since I never told myself that I was beautiful? I remember one guy I started dating in my early 20's told me I was gorgeous and looked like Angelina Jolie, so I dumped him immediately. Those words didn't reflect my inner world. I also realized that as soon as I started having kids, I never felt I ever had the time for anyone else in my life, so each man I found was never really available! They all were exact reflections of me. That's why they say you'll only allow the level of abuse that you'd give to your own self.]

"

True self-analysis is the greatest art of progress.

– Paramahansa Yogananda

"

Pay attention that you don't see your own face all day

☯ When you step out into nature, take a deep breath & say to yourself, "welcome to heaven." ♥ ♠

[I currently live on a busy street in front of my house and at the back of my house is a beautiful large river that we call the bird sanctuary. I can hear the rush of others' busy lives in the front of our house and see nature's peaceful, connected life in the back of our house. Every time I step out of the dense energy of my home to the vibrant, live energy of nature, no matter the weather, I say to myself or my kids, "welcome to heaven."]

☯ New habits create new neural pathways in the brain, aka new energy vibrations, that make change possible. ♥ ♠

☯ You do the same dance every day with the people in your life. You now need to become aware of what these dances are. What you're doing and be mindful of them to stop doing them. ♥ ♠

☯ I love going for a drive with my kids so we can all be together (be together and realize your own truths) ♥ ♠

"

*Eyes are the windows
to the soul.*

– William Shakespeare

☯ Your spirit's job now is to get to know your ego. And once this begins, the training starts. With gentle, non-judgemental awareness, your soul can only train your ego to speak and think with positive energy. The advantages are going to be awesome. ♡ ⬡

☯ Buddha said to laugh at yourself. Are you laughing? Laughing and crying are the exact same body movements. Shaking, breathing and tears. There are just different sounds. ♡ ⬡

Reframe your words (energy) from I'm trying to do this to; I'm doing this.

☯ Put down your phone. You need balance in your day. ♡ ⬡

☯ Pinpoint pain technique: Find any part of your body that's in pain, close your eyes and ask what the pain is saying. Try to find the exact location of the pain. See what happens. The pain cannot be pinpointed. ♡ ♠

☯ Train analogy: Imagine each lesson you learn in life is like hopping onto a train. (For example; a relationship) You get on the track in a circle. It's enjoyable initially, and the scenery is new and exciting. You are going around learning and growing, growing too big for the little train you're sitting in. Then the ride is over, and you know it's over, but you sit there anyway, desperately clinging to the feeling you had initially, and you won't let go. Then you start to suffer. You never know how big the train track circle will be, but the one thing you know and feel is when the ride (lesson) is over. Some lessons are significant, and some are small. They are all lessons. People are your teachers, and you are theirs. Which lessons in your current reality are over? ❶ ❷

❶ Sedona Method: Could you let them go? Yes. Would you let them go? Yes. When? NOW. ❶ ❷

Do something every day that speaks to your soul

❶ Yo Gamma Gamma Meditation: Close your eyes throughout the day. Stop rushing. Feed yourself with the breath of life. Calm your mind. Focusing on your breath will put your brain wave pattern into gamma, which can help improve your attention span. ❶ ❷

❶ Pay attention to the sunrise and sunset every day. Even if you only get a glimpse of the color from where you live. Say thank you for another day. ❶ ❷

Mindfulness in every single moment. No excuses. Excuses are what get in the way.

Create Good Karma

You are holding energy in your body in certain areas (chakras) that needs to be released.

❶ Time is a construct of the mind. Find out for yourself. ❶ ❷

[I have always been on time or early my entire life. I'd pride myself on this. Then one foggy morning driving the kids to school, we were late, and nothing happened! It was an even better "time" to drop the kids to school. I'm no longer going to be such a keeper of time.]

Walking in nature has a powerful effect on your energy and state of being. Walk in the woods looking for treasures without talking. Only listen to the birds singing to quieten your mind. Allow yourself to connect to the power and healing energy vibrations of the natural world around you. Nature assists in your body's natural ability to heal itself. ●●

Shrines are for your clues and treasures. Set one up for yourself. It can be anywhere. ●●

Wands are teaching you that you have the magic. You could use a beautiful stick that you find in nature as your wand. ●●

"

In the end, only three things matter: how much you loved, how gently you lived, and how gracefully you let go of things not meant for you.

- Buddha

"

When the mind becomes aware of what thoughts are, the body becomes aware of what food is. No diet is required. Everything in moderation. Eating colorful foods will increase your energy. Drinking tea throughout the day is a great way to increase your water intake. You can even put a tea bag in cold water, which will steep.

Push-ups are a fantastic way to build full-body strength. When you move your body, you get out of your head. Visualize a number in your mind, and you'll find that it will be the number of push-ups you reach. Start with one; it doesn't matter. Over time, you will increase the number naturally.

Hugs Heal. They regulate heart beats when your hearts are touching and regulate breathing, releasing oxytocin. Hug someone (even an animal) every day. It builds trust and safety and reduces your reactivity to perceived stress.

Your current lessons are your past lessons that you haven't learned yet. You need to discover your cycles (dances). That energy is trapped, and it will make you sick.

Godliness is next to cleanliness and cleanliness is next to Godliness

You cannot see the light without the darkness.

[Look up at a night sky and see the contrast. The stars are always there; even though you can't see them in the light of day.]

☯ Have a YES day! ♡ ⬥

☯ Earthing is a term for something I've been doing since I was a kid. Bare feet connecting to the ground were natural, something I didn't even consider. Try bare feet on the earth so the energy can go into your body. It's equivalent to taking handfuls of anti-oxidants except they absorb through the soles of your feet. (souls and soles sound a bit similar, don't they?) ♡ ⬥

What you do today affects your tomorrow and is a chain reaction. Just like you can't see a skyline at the water's edge through the mist, but you know it's there. You can't see your energy, but it's there, and you can't see your future, but it's there.

☯ Keep track of what your dreams are trying to tell you. ♡ ⬥

☯ When you wash your face or brush your teeth in the morning, look into your eyes in the mirror and tell yourself something that you love about yourself. ♡ ⬥

☯ Use your senses to ground yourself. ♡ ⬥

"

Power
to
the
peaceful

"

☯ Sun exposure is very important, and sun gazing opens your third eye. One evening during my sun gazing, I discovered that the sun is truly the colors of your third eye and crown chakras. Indigo and violet. ⬥ ⬥

☯ Slow dance with someone you love. Close your eyes. Enjoy. ⬥ ⬥

You can change your feelings with your thoughts

☯ Cold water therapy is highly beneficial for your immune system, and more. Take a cold shower at the end of your shower, and it's important to shower at the end of each day to rid your body of other's energy. Doing this will boost your immune system along with several other benefits. One thing I discovered that I found wasn't talked about much is that your body actually gets nice and hot after the cold-water shower. [I had a house full of sick people twice in a row. The first time was a sore throat, and the second time was a stomach bug. I didn't get sick once. The cold showers made my immune system stronger than ever. Resilience builds trust in yourself. You cannot think any thoughts during the cold-water therapy. Just breathe.] ⬥ ⬥

☯ Things you perceive as "good" or "bad" push you forward on your path. You move forward through the pain and the joy. Think back on all of your lessons. ⬥ ⬥

Currently, as a single mother of four, I'm not only living my reality but have four more realities joining mine daily. I laugh that Buddha, Jesus, Krishna & Lao Tzu weren't single parents. Sometimes I feel like a mother cat nursing her kittens, then they start to play, bite and pick at her, and she gets tired of it and puts them in their places with loving assuredness.

◐ As your day begins, ask what you need to learn today. Then at the end of your day, ask yourself if you planned any of the interactions and occurrences. Your life is unfolding naturally. Become aware of what you're learning here in Earth school daily. ♥ ♡

◐ Breathing renews your body, mind, and spirit. Practice box breathing to activate your sympathetic nervous system throughout the day. Breathe in for the count of four, hold for the count of 2, and breath out for the count of four. The breath can go anywhere in the body, to all cells. ♥ ♡

◐ Reframe unnecessary upset and worry with the question, will this matter five years from now? And then what will happen, asked over and over until you see the final outcome won't be as bad as you're imagining it to be. ♥ ♡

You need to embrace uncertainty to allow new incredible experiences to be drawn into your life like a magnet

◐ Write on your calendar; DAY 1 uncertainty. Do this every day for 7 days and see that it's okay. Every day is full of wonder, and you have choiceless awareness. ♥ ♡

At any moment you can walk away, drive away, fly away.

☯ Practicing silence. ⬡ ♡

Silence is my key to show the world a new teaching to become re-in-lightened. Daily vows of silence for one hour or more. A quieter world is a powerful world. United. Silence has been underrated and hidden. People love in silence. The world will open up and become one through the infinite space of silence. Power to the Peaceful. Universal consciousness. Love. No words. That's what we are. The silence in between the thoughts and words. What's left is peace and love. Connection. Universal Law. The most powerful one. You are the universe. Infinity. Now.

They say silence is golden. It is! Reclaim your power, and don't open your mouth to talk for as many hours as you can a day. Hit the mute button on yourself!

[I tried this for the first time in my life while writing this book. It was transformative, to say the least. It felt incredible. I felt it first in my 3rd chakra (power); it was like I was reclaiming my lost power. I then felt it in my 2nd chakra (emotions). It helped to make humming noises and chanting to release the energy. I realized after 6-hours daily for two days that I had a lot of pent-up inner rage. It was deep, rooted fear that I would be single forever, and I knew it wasn't true, that I would allow another to love me when I was ready. I spent so much of my time talking and convincing.

Most people thought my practicing silence was silly, crazy, saying; your kids need you (even though I was with them as usual), you're being too extreme, that was annoying and wondered when I was done with this. But these comments did not deter me. Silence was awakening me at the level of my gut. I heard more than ever before by simply not talking. I listened to what was inside me and what other people were really saying. There was no unnecessary chatter (energy) to fill the silence or reactions. No demands. I wasn't yelling and I was now leading with love in silence the more I practiced. People's words, actions, and projections didn't have as much as I thought to do with me. My silence made some people so angry & annoyed at me. But I didn't mind. When you're a spiritual warrior, that kind of stuff cannot faze you. When you let others talk, they reveal everything to you. I had no more useless, empty threats. I didn't always have to be heard, literally. My kids apologized for their behaviors without me demanding it. I also found that situations de-escalated very quickly. Others could see and hear their own behavior and words without mine. I discovered that I could communicate better than I thought with my energy and body language. I thought, do animals speak 12 hours a day? No, of course not, so why should we? I started to realize that I was talking too much, and when I did speak now, my words meant more. I used to be so proud of saying anything I wanted anytime with no filter but started to slowly learn the importance of silence. My kids listened to me more due to my silence too. Try this out for yourself. I love it so much that I made buttons to wear that say "I am currently practicing silence."] ☯ ⬣

☯ Get out and meet your life head-on! It would help to leave the safe cage you're fortunate to live in (home). Get out and explore your reality. But you are your own prisoner and jailer and hold the key. So, like a good pirate, get out and search for clues and messages to find your treasure. ☯ ⬣

☯ Say, I've been awake in this dimension since 5:30 a.m. Every morning, you rise again. ♥ ♠

☯ Create your own ecstatic dance party in your living room (just yourself or have others join). Put on some upbeat/happy music, close your eyes and let the music move you. ♥ ♠

☯ If you don't feel that you have the "time" to fit in a yoga class daily, you could always do what I like to call "all-day yoga." So, throughout the day, do a yoga pose and hold. ♥ ♠

"

To hear the silence of who you really are, you must first be silent.

– Jessgoodvibesonly

"

☯ Imagine the line past the F on a tank of gas. This is where your life can be now. Where have you been imagining your line to be set at? Empty? ♡ ♡

☯ Smell favorite smells multiple times a day. [For me, it's the smell of my kid's hair, freshly cut grass, incense, coffee, essential oils, campfire, clothes off the line and more. Pay attention to your own] ♡ ♡

☯ Hold hands with someone you love. Your palms are the maps of your soul. ♡ ♡

You could be a bit broken or completely broken, it doesn't matter because the only one who can put you back together is yourself.

☯ Jump face down onto a soft bed with abandon like you would have done as a kid! Then roll over and stretch out. ♡ ♡

☯ Throughout your day, sink down into your heart center to be in the moment. Put your hand on your chest to connect even deeper and breathe in love. ♡ ♡

☯ Rather than focus on how you've been perceiving someone else to be failing in their life, pay attention to yourself first. As the saying goes, you can lead a horse to water, but you cannot make them drink. You need to lead yourself there and do what you need to do. They may or may not follow by example. And that's alright. Everyone is on their own unique path. Focus on your own with honesty, patience, and love. ♥ ♦

Your daily re-enlightenment path can change directions at any time since the path is not linear and time is a construct of the mind

☯ Layers of sound meditation. Go outside if you can and listen to all the layers of different sounds while meditating. Close your eyes, breathe, and listen. ♥ ♦

☯ New morning rituals are critical to see a change in your life because when you create new habits, you forge new neural pathways in your brain. For example, change your mug to something that makes you feel joy.. ♥ ♦

Grounding is to let go. So, you can let go when you put your feet on the ground and connect to the earth. Let go to rise to your heights.

☯ You want to get to the next moment when you're half paying attention to someone. Then, when you can fully pay attention to yourself first, and only then can you can give that to others and not want to escape to the next moment. Try it. ♥ ♦

☯ Nose breathing alternating nostrils. ♥ ♦

☯ If you think people don't change, close your eyes and think of the people you've been at all your different ages and times in your life. ◐
♡

☯ Train yourself to stop and pause before you react with the same of body reactions. In most cases, you need to do the opposite of what you usually do. ◐ ♡

☯ Cinderella knew she had everything she ever needed and had gratitude in her heart. She was then rewarded and became the princess. She also believed in true love and a fairy tale ending. So she cleaned, and cleanliness is next to godliness. Not just for your body but also for your home. When you clean your home and take pride in every belonging, you will see magical changes in your life. What did Bradley Cooper do in the movie Limitless? The first thing he did was clean his apartment. That says it all.

The power of gratitude to create abundance. When you empty a room, the possibilities are endless. Clean your rooms in categories or sections, leaving only the things you love, that spark joy as Marie Kondo says. ◐ ♡

Let go of self-judgment and competition. Competition is not real. It gives the illusion of division. Remember that there's room for everyone because we are all one.

I knew I was waking up when that voice in my head kept saying my wrinkles are ugly; you need to hide them... stopped, and I now feel they are beautiful. My ego voice was dissolving, and I felt more connected to everything.

"

I shall not commit the fashionable stupidity of regarding everything I cannot explain as a fraud.

– C.G. Jung

"

☯ To feel the power of your words and know they are energy vibrating while you speak, gently touch your throat. ◐ ◑

☯ Swing on a swing like you would have as a kid. Close your eyes. Relax. ◐ ◑

☯ Posture is crucial to connect to the source and channel. Your belly button is your power. Stand straight and connect. ◐ ◑

☯ Travelling takes you outside of your created comfort zone and habits. Travel to expand your mind. ◐ ◑

☯ Go outside and let the wind blow "through you," cleansing your energy. ◐ ◑

☯ Maslow's dog bell and our phone ding notifications are the same. Every time you hear the bell, you get a dopamine hit because they want to diminish your dopamine receptors and the amount of chemicals you have available. Adrenaline and cortisol are released (fight/flight/freeze) when you get a negative message, burning you out and creating depression/anxiety. Serotonin, dopamine, and oxytocin are released to make you happy. You will never wake up with all these constant chemical releases creating chaos. You are either in heaven or hell, here in the NOW. It's not a place to get to. The choice is up to you. Shut off your notifications to save yourself. ◐ ◑

☯ Go out into the wind and practice feeling like the magnet that you are. Let the wind touch your face or arms, and imagine you are a magnet attracting every thought and feeling. Like attracts like. Your outside world is a reflection of your inner world. ◐ ◑

☯ You can do it too! I now have my monkey mind trained and listening to me rather than me listening to my monkey mind. Every emotion and thought on a whim, ever-changing to quietly contemplating every moment and being aware. Awareness is the key. (You can imagine any animal that resonates with you to replace the monkey.) ☯ ⬤

☯ Zoom out meditation: Imagine yourself where you are on the planet and zoom out into outer space to see the perspective of how tiny your imagined problems and limitations are. ☯ ⬤

Be like a dog, excited about life!

☯ Don't be offended by someone's energy or "armor/mask." You are transparent and let it go through you. ☯ ⬤

☯ When you think or feel that someone is defensive or stubborn, it's actually you. Remember that this person is holding up a mirror. That's why they say; you are reflected in someone else's eyes. That's where you see the mirror. ☯ ⬤

☯ Every moment is BRAND NEW meditation. ☯ ⬤

With each tick of a clock for a second that passes, everything, including yourself, is brand new. Each sound, breath, feeling, thought, and sight is new.

☯ Repeat the sentence – I will be well. (positive words only) ☯ ⬤

☯ Listen to sad songs. I always disliked sad songs up until now. I can understand the power of a sad song. It makes you do things from your heart. ♥ ◔

Observation and Sensing
YOU ARE HERE
released
imagination!
BELIEVE
third
EYE.
discoveries
CHANGE
BREATHE
LIVE
STAR
LIGHT, its EYES
ENERGY
long dreamed
live
humans.
INNER
SURPRISING.

A QUICK DAILY GUIDE

Meditate daily. No excuses, like you're training. Meditate sitting comfortably if you need to, just get started.

Go bare feet on the earth so the energy can go into your body. (Grass and earth, not pavement.)

Take a cold shower at the end of your shower, and it's essential to shower others' energy off your body daily.

Do box breathing to activate your vagus nerve. For example, in for 4, hold for 2, out for 4.

Do push-ups daily.

Create new morning rituals.

Truth and lies. (Remember)

Sway test.

Get as much sunshine as possible.

Use your senses to bring you back into the present moment.

The screen saver on your phone and turn off unnecessary notifications.

Close your eyes for a moment throughout the day. Pause.

Laugh.

Remember that Thanks-Giving is everyday.

Hug someone you love.

Stop rushing. Bring your awareness into your body's tension. Relax.

A Spiritual Warrior's Path

Podcast jessgoodvibesonly on Podbean. These are my diaries from 2020.

AWAKENING and homesteading

In this episode, I'm going to talk about awakening and homesteading.

With all that's been going on in the world, I can't help but stay optimistic. Not optimistic that things will go back to how they were but optimistic that we can handle this new way of living. This is an awakening for the world. We needed to hit the stop button. It is time to look around you and realize what's important. I know I am doing this and it's my kids and my family. I've been preparing for this without knowing when or how it would come. I have books on how to live a self-sufficient life and started my first garden last year. I know what I need to live off the land. You don't have to live in the country or need sprawling acres. You could start with a box garden, a compostable toilet, rain barrels, chickens, hens, and solar panels for a start. It's time to embrace cooking at home. I'm so thankful that I've been cooking since a very young age but it's never too late to start. It's fantastic for my kids that they have one another to play with and lucky for them, I've been setting up our backyard park for years.

Remember too that, and I can't stress it enough... you need to remain positive. Don't get sucked into people's or your own negativity. It's easier to go there but don't. Your body will vibrate at a lower frequency, and you will get sick. Stay positive and accept your new way of living. And now that I'm back to homeschooling, we have a beautiful group of friends that share the same values.

Here is a poem that I wrote at the beginning of this "pandemic":

Awakening

Chaos, static, feverishly
Spinning out of control.
Now quiet, calm, slowing, peaceful.
Go inward. Pause. Reassess.
Days are now more meaningful.
Colors brighten as the days pour slowly like
Liquid honey.
The world had to stop.
Constant pushing, striving, searching.
Bigger, better, more.
To accepting, yielding, restful, and ease.
Meaning in meaningless things
Fall away.
Open your eyes,
You see the way.

Island Roots Homestead

This is a dream & vision of mine that I've had for years. I would like this to happen in 2021. As a mom, know that this way of living, is the future. Teaching our children how to live off the land.

I want our homestead to be an experience for people to visit. This will be for those who crave a connection to the earth and their community. Homesteading is a viable solution, and Island Roots Homestead will support a life centered around self-sufficiency and connection to our land in Prince Edward Island.

I want to teach my children and visitors how to live off the land the way islanders once did. With gardens and small animal livestock, visitors will have the chance to learn how a homestead works. We will cook a meal together using ingredients from the farm or locally sourced when needed.

Dating and Jaded

Perseverance, determination and manifesting your reality.

In this episode, I'm going to talk about how I became a makeup artist and how my makeup school.

Paramita Academy of Makeup Inc. has evolved. And as cliché as it sounds, it's 2020 and I'm looking back and moving forward

My year so far has been the worst year of my life. My makeup school seemed to be over because I lost my Toronto branch owner, and I couldn't travel from where I live in Prince Edward Island due to teach in Toronto due to Covid. But that was the least of my worries when my identical twin sister in Toronto was in psychosis (something I knew nothing about but learned about very quickly) and she was a missing person in Canada on top of that. This made my entire life to date look like a walk in the park and I'm a single mom, so as you can imagine I've been through my share of ups and downs. Well, I guess this story is a whole other podcast in itself.

I want to talk about how I took the most negative things that were happening to me and decided to focus on myself, my kids, and my business. What a concept, to put others aside and only think of your own life. I had to and did, look at the positives in my life and I was the owner of an amazing makeup school that I created in 2002. I was a makeup artist since 1999 and I wasn't going to let that fade away. I had to breathe new life into something that I created on my own. So, I started to research and decided to make the best of my situation and made my school into an online platform. I worked harder than ever and created my instructional videos. It was the best experience and I realized how much I still loved doing makeup and I renewed my love of teaching.

I downloaded an audio book by Tony Robbins. I never listed to him before. He was transformative! Did his information ever make a change in my life! He taught how; you have to ask yourself the right questions. – I was asking myself; why am I not getting any students? And my mind would give me a stupid answer: because no one wants to go to your school anymore. And then I started asking the right questions; how can I get more students? And I answered; pay someone to update my social media and website.

I then started by, asking for help. Something I don't do often. I looked to a social media expert, Cassandra with Inspire Social Studios to take over my Instagram page for a month. She took one look at my out-of-date website and sent me to an awesome website developer, Stephanie with Summer Street Creative, who created exactly what I had in mind. My vision was classic, black, and white, and it was mobile friendly… my old website was not. Plus, apparently, I had way too much writing on it, back in 2001 when I launched my site, the internet was relatively new. People had desktop computers and spent more than 30 seconds looking at a website. I cut to the chase and only included relevant information for my potential students to read along with endless testimonials, those were something I cherished and couldn't leave out. I'm so proud of those words, and thankful. My school has 20 5-star reviews on google and 5 stars everywhere else too. Something I take great pride in.

My makeup school has evolved over the years, as much as I have really. I became a makeup artist in London, England at the very young age of 19. My twin sister and I spend close to a month in England, Scotland, Spain, and Morocco a year before that. So maybe this trip made me feel brave enough to venture overseas from the east coast of Canada alone to attend school. I remember finding the ad in the back of a fashion magazine. Delamar Academy of Makeup. Become a makeup artist. Funny thing was, I wasn't even that into makeup then. I don't know now what I was thinking then. I was naturally artistic but wasn't even wearing much makeup. I spent a month at school. I remember hanging from a strap on the tube, commuting an hour each direction everyday. I was one of the top students in my class. I loved the teachers, and they loved me! I still remember their names. James Anda and Charmaine Fuller. I was homesick and my twin and friend at the time came to visit me and after my course, I returned home with them. Upon arriving back on Prince Edward Island, I was lucky enough to be the only makeup artist in my province. Imagine that?! I was a big fish in a little pond. I had an article written about me in the newspaper and had the chance to do makeup on Peter Mansbridge from CBC's the National along with musicians and well-known TV reporters. I decided to move to Montreal and worked with fashion photographers and then on to Toronto where I worked with more photographers for the National Film Centre. I even had the chance to do makeup for the TV show Look-a-like on the cast. I was on the show getting made over as Nicole Richie when they found out that I was a makeup artist. My career seemed to take off from the start. I loved doing makeup and my confidence was growing. I moved back to Prince Edward Island and decided that I wanted more. I remember getting a letter in the mail (imagine that... before texts and emails were mainstream) from a woman asking me if there were any schools in PEI to teach makeup. Her daughter was interested, and the mom saw my article in the paper. I'm a bit of a big dreamer, so I thought, I'll open my own school. I spent over a year creating my curriculum, getting approved by the province to license my school, a teaching license, get incorporated, create my website, and open my location. It was a challenge, and I had my setbacks, but I moved forward. Determined and confident with what I had to offer. My school opened October 2002 and I had a full class! I had a huge Halloween costume party with a band and a caterer to launch. I was cleopatra! What a night to remember. My dream came true. I then had the chance to do makeup on Chef Michael Smith for the Food Network series Chef at Home and do makeup on Ellen Page. My school started to slow down on the East Coast, even though it was the only makeup school east of

Montreal. I decided to make a huge move on my own and moved back to Toronto to launch my school there. In 2005, my only competition was one other makeup school in the city. It started off slow. I took a course in hypnotherapy for fun and my teacher happened to be a famous psychic from England. Yvonne Oswald. She did a reading for me and some of you may or may not believe in psychics, but I do. She gave me the best advice for my school and told me to shorten my program and call it a bootcamp. I created a one-week course. I removed outdated lessons. My course included special effects makeup and I just wanted to concentrate on beauty, fashion, and bridal makeup. My school took off again! My personal journey along the way is a complete other story. I'll tell you another time and I'll try to stick to how my school has evolved. I read many books to learn about the power of my mind and I believe this helped with my school. I went to the millionaire mind, read How to Get from Where You Are to Where You Want to Be by Jack Canfield, The Power Of Now by Eckhart Tolle, The Secret and probably 30 more books like this. I was the only instructor at my school up until 2011. I spent 8 years going it alone and then one of my students named Grace King suggested that I branch out, so I did. I created branch locations and gave my Paramita graduates the opportunity to open their own schools for free. They just had to send me commission from each of their students. I had branches in Dubai, Medicine Hat, Toronto, Ottawa, New York, and Port Hope. They were all amazing and kept their locations going for as long as it suited them. It seemed that most of them became mothers, and their schools took a back seat. They all slowly faded but I enjoyed the ride and learned a lot. Just this year, 2020 as I'm telling you this and looking back on my career and my life, I'm back at it alone. It's me that I'm selling now as the owner and only instructor to my students. I'm going to continue to move forward and as my school's name says Paramita, it means in Sanskrit; having reached the goal... I've done that but I have more goals and I know I'll reach them all.

Powerful manifester and looking back, I was only 22 when I opened my school. I created notes and images of what it would be like to own a makeup school before Pinterest or vision boards even existed. I created my reality.

Tony Robbins... you can't keep doing the same thing and expect to get different results. One night no milk and peaceful sleeps... they say it takes you the length of your relationship halved to get over it... so you do the math, and it will be worth it.

How to become a doer

My advice as an entrepreneur would be:

Be a doer, just start. Be genuine & real, honest & kind.

Surround yourself with people who believe in you but sometimes this isn't easily done. If you hear any negativity, ignore it. It's not you, it's them. If they keep slinging the negativity and doubt at you. Keep quiet and reach your dreams and visions in silence. You don't need to share it all. Show yourself. Know your worth and know the why behind your reach for success. Stand behind what's important to you.

My advice

No matter your story, background, or beliefs at the heart of it, we are all connected. We all long for love. The feelings of peace, joy, and happiness. The truth is that these are there inside of us all, the light. If you can change your life so that you can live a real and authentic one that you can look back on and remember fondly, then do it. You are given each day as a gift, the present moment. Change happens in the little things that you do daily. The past is gone, and the future is yet to unfold. Ask yourself if you are settling for less. Run towards your wildest dreams. Get outside and sit with yourself. The wind will whisper the answers that you already know deep inside. Love yourself and listen. Claim your true self. We are all souls on our own journeys. You need to choose the ones to be by your side that bring you light. You'll know when their souls are vibrating at the same frequency as yours.

We wrote everything that needed to be said. Of course, there's always more, but that's all we feel the need to share. We can't even tell you how hard it was to decide to write the truth. For fear of hurting anyone. They say the truth will set you free. We feel like everyone has a story to tell and everyone craves for someone to listen. We will tell our stories, until they are that, just stories. Not emotional attachments in our bodies, energy with words written, read, and released. To help people in some way to see life is not perfect and yes, you need to be positive to open and grow, but sometimes that does mean letting things and people go along the way. Everyone teaches you something, or you teach them something. Karma and your path are yours alone. You won't be saving anyone from themselves. Saving yourself is up to you.

We all make mistakes in life, so why is choosing the wrong partner such a taboo mistake? We don't want to be another statistic added to the pile of divorces in our culture. So instead, we hide the mistake or try to make it look like we didn't make one at all. Don't let your mistake be your life; that is much worse. It takes bravery and strength to do something about a bad decision. Trust me, life goes on after the mistake has been rectified and people get over the initial shock of you admitting it. After all, most people are concerned with their own lives and only wish you happiness in the end. Plus, they are busy re-evaluating their own marriages when they see one so close to theirs fail.

Don't let the opinions of others determine the course of your life. It's simple: if you are unhappy, become happy. If it means taking a stance and taking charge of your life, do it. Or at least try. You are your own best friend. Would you want your best friend to be treated with anything but respect and kindness? Would you want your best friend to be happy or unhappy? Choose happiness.

You really need to stand your ground and make decisions based upon your honest gut feelings. Stick to the decisions and don't allow outside influences or guilt cause you to waver. Remember that deep roots don't fear the wind.

Don't let people influence you too heavily into thinking and believing what they believe is right. You can listen to their advice, but it doesn't mean you have to follow it. By listening and letting yourself think about what they said you can feel whether or not it is valid advice for you.

Change is life and life is change. Everyone is doing the best they can with what they know.

Charlie Brown: "You only live once."

Snoopy: "False. You live everyday. You only die once."

From the start you cannot let anyone get comfortable with disrespecting you, and you need to be careful with what you tolerate since you're teaching that person how to treat you. If you're not aware of how many times you "let things slide" then they will continue in this way. Set healthy boundaries. But you can't set these boundaries until you respect and love yourself first. People can slip up and say and do things that they regret. But 'sorry' only works if it's followed by action and changed behaviour. Otherwise, 'sorry' just becomes a word. If it's overused, it becomes even less than that.

†Jess: What would I say to my younger self? I guess that you are lonely and desperate to have someone love you. You have to love yourself first, dear girl. You should stop searching for your "other half." I guess you'll have to live and learn, though, and it's usually the hard way. You never listen to

anyone anyway. You think that you've found someone to take away your loneliness, but you will realize that you must learn how to be alone first. You are strong and have always been this way. You should be honest with yourself and take time when making decisions. You will have the courage to walk away when you need to, though, in the end. When your head fights with your heart, only listen to your heart. I forgive you for believing in true love. For being optimistic and hopeful. Hoping for change. Loving someone despite their faults. Trying. Forgiving and forgetting so easily. Playing a role. Getting walked on. Paying for everything. Never giving up.

For all those overthinkers out there... You sometimes just have to throw it out into the universe and Fate will catch it. Let it go, especially if you want to cling desperately. Life works out in its ways and only in looking back can we see that. Power to the peaceful and try to remember that you are a spiritual being having a human experience.

LET GO

Wade out into the water
Look at the vastness
And stillness of the horizon
Breathe as the earth breathes
The air fills your lungs
As the waves lap against you
The incessant waves that never stop
Like your thoughts
Sometimes they calm
Like the glass surface
But the waves still gently lap in
Your mind can never truly be still
All you can do is listen and let go.

My twin, running away and my spiritual journey

Being from a small province on the east coast of Canada with a population of 138,000 in 1998, we always dreamt of bigger and better things. Little did we know, lost among Toronto's big city lights, that we would spend years longing to be back on an island that we called home.

One summer at our grandparents' cottage, we were introduced to our father's cousin. She was a glamourous opera singer who lived in London, England. She casually invited us for a trip overseas to see her and we jumped at the chance. Imagine, twin girls, only 18 years old with no cell phones or Internet and our mom's credit card, alone in Europe for the first time.

We were lucky enough to see our cousin sing at the Royal Opera House in Covent Garden. Hanging out in her dressing room, we felt a world away from home. Walking out the doors onto the cobblestone streets of London we felt then that there was so much more out there for us to see.

To add to our adventure, we braved the streets of London to a place called Metal Morphosis where a guy completely covered in tattoos and body piercings held a gun up to our stomachs and he pierced our navels. We couldn't only visit London, so we travelled up along the coast to Scotland then back down across England to the sunny palm- tree lined shores of St. Ives. We saw a vacation package commercial on TV at our B&B and booked a flight to Spain. We didn't stop there, we yelled through the streets of Spain that we were going to Africa! We took a tour and a ferry-boat ride by the Rock of Gibraltar to Morocco. We were foolish young girls and didn't even have a Dirham in our pockets to get a bottle of water. An older couple on the tour felt sorry for us and offered some red wine while at dinner, when all we desperately wanted was water. While getting a ride on a camel, then a donkey, a young boy with two palms wide open pushed our bums up onto the animal. Vendors would constantly harass us to buy their handmade goods. Since we didn't have any money, we would laugh and offer them a few Pesetas and ask is this enough to buy that? This would turn them away quickly. We thought of ourselves as clever and worldly at such a young age.

†Jess: With a passion and new-found love of travelling we would settle back home to study travel and tourism management together. A year of schooling would go by, but things would change when I found an article at the back of a fashion magazine and cut it out. To the shock and surprise of my twin, I decided to venture off alone to become a makeup artist in London, England at the young age of 19. Thanks to the support of our stepdad and mom. Being alone was a foreign thought and feeling. This was the fork in our path, the decision that would change our world; our lives together as twins would soon end. Our wanderlust passion would burn on, though. Ever since then I travelled to 22 countries and my twin travelled to 11.

How many times could we "run away"? I lived in 20 different apartments in three different provinces hoping to find happiness with each move. I drove across Canada with two guys I met from France while waitressing. I quiet my job days later and joined them. I was seen as wild and free, and I didn't care what anyone though about me. I was having fun! My twin told me while writing our memoirs together, that she was so envious of my freedom and all my adventures. I had no idea at the time because she was so critical and judgemental of me. But only because she had to hide how she really felt since she was "happily married". I spent my winters in Mexico and Thailand for six years. In the process of writing this book, reflecting on my life, I've come to realize that I've been running away for a very long time now, almost my entire life. My twin had a dream that she was talking to a man about our book, and she told him "Jess traveled all over the world and lived in many places but in the end, she was happiest where she started. Back in her grandmother's backyard with her kids."

Jess: My search for myself started after twin left me, in my early 20s. I was given my first self-help books from one of my first students, The Invitation and The Call by Oriah Mountain Dreamer. I also started doing yoga. I can remember my first class like it was yesterday. I can smell the incense in the room and feel the cool fall air as I walked to class from my first loft apartment that I lived in alone. Next, I'd read the book Siddhartha by Hermann Hesse. Over the years I had a cleansing done by a Shamanic healer in Mexico City and was blessed by a Buddhist Monk in Thailand. I was hypnotized, learned to practice hypnosis, have been to psychics and have had a past life regression done. I visited orphanages in Mexico and create products to raise money to donate. I also found an eagle feather on the beach one summer. Finding an eagle feather meant that I was on a higher spiritual path. Given my Mi'kmaq heritage, this was incredibly meaningful to me.

Before my husband at the time got kicked out of the country, we found out about "The Secret". After that, I listened to Oprah & Eckhart Tolle's podcasts of "A New Earth". Followed by "The Power of Now", "The Success Principles", Deepak Chopra's books, "I Can Make You Happy" and "The Monk Who Sold his Ferrari", "The Celestine Prophecy", OSHO, "4 Agreements" and more. I went on to complete two levels of Reiki energy healing.

All of this kept our marriage together even longer. I was learning how to live in the now and forgive. Michael Singer's book "Untethered Soul" was my last book to read while we were in Thailand, and it helped me through some of the hardest times in my life.

All along I was in the process of trying to heal myself and I thought I could heal him and our marriage. I learned that you cannot heal another person if they don't want you to, but I am grateful that these books have helped me to heal.

From the books that I've read, I've learned that I built my mental model or ego on avoiding pain. This started in childhood, and I'd say that I was trying to protect myself against abandonment. With all the fighting to protect myself against this, I 'got' it. I was focusing all my energy here, only to have my twin abandon me then to have my husband abandon me, too.

Co-writing my memoirs with my twin sister has had a significantly positive impact on my path to healing. I can't stress enough the importance of writing your life story. I will be forever thankful to all these authors, gurus, and teachers.

Just as a plant grows fresh new green leaves and sheds the old ones, yellow and dying below... you must grow. And just as a flower turns into a berry you must evolve.

In this section, I'm going to talk about fitting it all in and social media.

People ask me how I fit it all in. Running a business from home, cooking, keeping up with social media, podcasting, taking care of 3 kids while homeschooling, reading tons of books while still maintaining a social life. For me, the answer is... I don't sit still. I feel like, you only have one life. Once chance to make the most of it. But when it all comes down to it, you don't just have one life, you have one day, this day. So, I don't want to lie in bed at night and think, what a waste of a day. I did nothing. Maybe I'm too far in one direction and don't have a balance. But when you're happy doing what you're doing, it's easy to be like this. I find joy in doing the things I love. I've always reached for more.

I tried traditional therapy this year for the first time and won't be going back actually. She told me a bunch of things that I already knew, and she told me to sit still. Find balance but to be honest. That's the toughest thing for me to do. I don't watch TV and when I do, all I can think about is how I'd rather be living my life rather than watching some actors live theirs on screen.

I'm not going to paint you this perfect picture though. My house is messy with toys and laundry. I'd be embarrassed to have someone stop over without notice most days. But I'd rather a messy house now and happy kids. I'm a single mom, so there are perks that come with that. I don't have to have the house looking like a magazine and dinner on the table anymore. My friend Erica taught me that we are all just managing stuff. So, I've been donating the stuff we don't need or use anymore. I found myself shoveling Legos and toys with a plastic shovel, indoors the other day. I was laughing and thinking to post a meme asking people if they find themselves shoveling plastic too?

So, here's some advice on how to get it all done. Get up early and go to bed early. I love to cook in the morning too. Get it over with early, not when you're tired in the evening. Write lists on paper of the things you need to get done. The ones that are bothering you. And chip away at it. Don't get bills in the mail. Get automatic withdraws from your account. Whatever you take into the house, try to take something out. Make space. Don't have too many clothes. Just 5 outfits per person. Only store leftovers on the bottom shelf in your fridge, so they don't get lost.

Another thing... Don't stare at your phone... and here's something I wrote regarding this topic last year:

: My plan was to take one month off social media, dating apps, planning trips, and trying to find a man. I had my dominoes lined up and I knocked them all down on purpose. My phone was a false connection to the outside world. I wasn't going to participate and wanted to take the time to see what would actually happen if I stopped searching and reaching out. This was my time to retreat inwards and find some peace within myself and restore my energy. I needed to look at the areas of my life in a new way. I was hoping to let go of habits and beliefs that were clearly not working for me. It's as though we have an innate instinct to search for a partner.

After only a day of being disconnected I have a feeling of empowerment. I am more productive because I'm not checking my phone every few minutes. My addiction to my phone was getting so bad that I was looking at it in the middle of the night and waking up too early to check if anyone had taken the time to write me.

Not having any trips planned, aka not running away was proving to be the toughest one to stick to for me. It honestly shouldn't feel so difficult to not plan a trip considering I just got back from a two-week trip to Toronto, and I was already thinking about taking a trip to Portugal. The feeling I get from having a vacation planned gives me a sense of excitement and hope for something better to come, so not having this was very difficult for me.

If I ask myself why I post so many pictures, I think it's because I want to show people that I spend a lot of time doing fun things alone with my three kids. I'm happy, for real. Maybe I was showing people that they could be doing these things with me. Or was I showing people that I don't need anyone else to do these things with?

Throughout the day I find myself to be angry and over-reactive to everything and anyone in my path because I need my fix, my phone. I'm also cranky, frustrated, and annoyed. Wow, that device was more of an addiction than I realized! This is not good. I'm constantly looking to pick it up to see what I'm missing or who liked my pictures or wrote to me. I had a secret joy hoping someone would write when I didn't expect it, a little present just for me.

I needed to reclaim my power. To stand alone. I'm finally willing to give myself over to my solitude.

After a long day goes by and I don't look at my phone, it feels like I'm not allowed to open a wrapped present. I feel detached by not looking at social media and it makes me want to take a step back from any unhealthy friendships. I can see how cell phones can ruin relationships, when you're sitting there on your phone instead of engaging with one another.

I have been so much more productive. Wow, getting things done. Not constantly looking at my phone for a "break". Also, I've been living in the moment more, not looking at my phone and pretending to be in the moment. I've already started taking less pictures with my phone and I started taking more with my memory instead.

Well, Day One felt like a month ago. I didn't wake up on Day Two as early because I knew I wasn't allowed to check my phone. So, I got some writing done instead. I'm getting so much done that it's safe to say that if you're not getting stuff done in your life, you can blame your phone, hence you can blame yourself.

Subliminally I saw this message the day before I started this challenge. A mindfulness magazine that my son placed facing forward in our bookshelf said on the front "Put your phone down." I've been looking in the wrong places for genuine joy and a deeper connectedness in my life. I am committed to this well-needed change.

I'm going to go with the flow of my life, watching how things unfold without my forcing it. I do trust that this will lead me to my goal. I'm going to trust this process. I'll spend some time in silence, away from the crowd. I will not hold onto things just because they're there. There is no longer room in my life for familiar emotional patterns or negative thought processes. I will let go.

I realized that once I set my mind to something, I could do anything. My days felt more fulfilled, and I realize, how was I supposed to be living in the moment when my cell phone was constantly taking me out of every moment? It's like I couldn't take my eyes off the faces, colours, pictures, words, and constant newness of social media.

There's gotta be more to life than focusing on your weight, paying your bills, searching for connections, checking your phone, and caring about what other people think.

I'm finding myself more patient now. Like my days are longer and I have lots of time to fit it all in. I'm finishing up my Neuro Linguistic Programming course online. I seemed to never have had the time for that before. I also started reading again and finished The Alchemist by Paulo Coelho in one night. Next was Life After Death by Deepak Chopra.

I just found out that staring at my phone and social media releases dopamine. It controls desire. It tells you when you want something and compels you to get it. It pushes you to keep talking, pushing, or scrolling. And each time you do, Dopamine sends more pleasure signals to the brain. It's a dangerous cycle because the longer you let it go on, the harder it is to break. Social media became the stage that I could not get off of. I was no longer going to participate or volunteer my time. Plus, no one was as they say; blowing up my phone. No men were contacting me anyway. I was doing all the writing and once that stopped, it all stopped. What a waste of time!

It's like I imagine it out of an old classic cartoon. The little devil or ego or unconsciousness is sitting on one shoulder and the little angel, or your soul or consciousness is sitting on the other shoulder. The devil is yelling at you to pick up your old habits, having you defend yourself to others, gossiping, complaining, worrying and the list goes on. But your angel whispers. It's easier to hear the loudness of your thoughts. You must stop and breathe and take a seat with the angel. Listening but not acting. Being aware. Your thoughts will always be there, so don't try to fight the little devil because it will only give it power. It will in turn make you feel more powerful when you act on all the things it says. Leaving you drained in the end. There's always a price with the devil. So, each time you must choose to sit with the angel and there is where you will find your peace. Only in your awareness each day, every day. Gratitude, hope, joy, inspiration, affection, enthusiasm, optimism, happiness, and love.

I'd love to say that I followed through with this promise to myself. But I would be lying if I said that. After four days off social media, I checked my Instagram messages and didn't see a reply from a person that I was waiting awhile to hear back from. So, I blocked him and logged out. Then after a week of no social media, I went out with an old school friend. She was inviting people to join us, and I logged back on, to do the same. Then I decided to check my Facebook for a minute and saw three new friend requests. Man, do I ever suck at doing what I said I'd do. Plus, to make this worse, I didn't plan a trip, I just packed up the same day and took my three kids off the Island to have some summer fun. I did say no planning trips, so maybe this one didn't count? Maybe my promises were exaggerated. I might just cut back on all of these things but cutting them all out for a month seems to be unrealistic.

If I am honest with myself, I want to change men or help them. I've yet to find a real emotional connection with someone who can actually date me. Uh, here we go again... It's like I'm going against nature. Against my human instinct to connect with another. It's "that time of the month" again where being alone is a struggle inside my body and mind. All the other days, I could care less if there was someone by my side. But right now, I find myself searching and looking for someone as a partner. But this time when I want a partner, the feeling is fleeting, lasting only a few days at best and then I'm back to being fiercely independent again.

Well, I have a week left to my challenge. I couldn't care less now if I looked at Instagram or Facebook again. I discovered that being on the internet was an energy drain like a vacuum. As the summer came to an end, the cool air was forcing me to retreat indoors, and I've been reading non-stop. I finished reading The Untethered Soul by Michael Singer and am currently reading Calling Us Home by Chris Luttichau. In the last week I found that it helps to replace old habits with new healthier ones. Reading and writing happened to be mine. In writing and learning all that I have, I've become so much stronger than I've ever imagined was possible.

I'm in LOVE with ME!

After this month... I booked a trip to Portugal with my childhood friend Chantel so I could meet up with a friend I made while in Italy the year before. I will be stopping in Toronto to see my twin for the day and will meet her new baby girl. I went on a few dates and stayed mindful about being on social media too much.

LET YOURSELF FLY — I wrote this when I was 21, living alone in Toronto.

Find the peace within
Then will life truly begin
What is meant to be
Will be

All you have is this moment
And that moment just past,
Stop looking into the future
Time will go by too fast

Don't look back and wish
You had lived for the moment
And spent more time
With the ones you now miss

Life is full of sorrow
Beauty and pain
You need to let go
Or there will be nothing to gain

Don't let the dark keep you
Instead let the light take you
Follow the good
Knowing in life
You did all that you could

Love
And be loved
Feel free like the angels
And let yourself fly
Live life to its fullest
Then you can die

THE RIVERS

The rivers run deep
Like veins through the woods
Like us, as we travel through life
Never staying the same
Forever changing

We will meet and love
As we travel along
But the time will come
Too soon to see
When our friendship's
Just a memory

Our time together
Will suddenly end
No more days for us
Together to spend

We didn't see it coming.
It was around the trees.

As we travel through life
Everyone must leave

And if through our journeys.
We find ourselves lost.
Our parting in life
Would be the cost

Just look back and remember.
The times that we've had
And if you feel alone
It's okay to be sad

Because the rivers
Will meet again sometime
And we'll travel together
You and I

❦ Jess 2001

Looking back over my life, my perceived bad experiences have shaped me into the person I am now. The earliest memory of my childhood would be, getting picked up from daycare. It was dark out, in the wintertime. I sat in the back seat of my dad's truck next to my twin sister. My parents were newly divorced, and we were going to spend a week with our dad. I wanted my mom. The sad song on the radio still brings back sad memories from 1984, as Oh Sherrie by Steve Perry played, I cried silently in the backseat.

"It doesn't get easier, you get stronger"

- Kids almost dying

- Car accidents
- Ex-husband not arriving in Madrid to meet me
- Not being able to enter Thailand
- Ex-husband getting kicked out of the country
- Moving 20-something times
- Twin missing
- Getting divorced twice
- Living alone
- Getting skin cancer
- Two divorces
- Being pregnant and single at the same time
- My twin sister not in my life
- Going to school in England alone when I was only 19
- Parents almost dying
- Grandparents dying

In uncovering your unconscious, you may discover that in life, sometimes you really do feel like a nut, and sometimes you don't. But what else can you do but crack it open and see what's inside? As strong as you are, you need to find a balancing act. You were born to be bold because you are growing bolder, not older. So spread the love and see why life improves with the healing power of friendships and love. Feel more and surround yourself with people who only lift you higher. Because you have a blooming lovely soul!

Just say yes, yes to the world. Make your dream a reality. Power to the peaceful. There's always a challenge to work towards. Where's your gratitude meter set? Start with feeling good; this is your year to renew. To explore. To grow. Up, up, up. Take a leap of faith. Ignite something. Get a new, improved way of seeing. Focus on your inner life with meditation and positive thinking. Make it happen because it's about time! Go for the bold! See the wonderful, listen up! The soul is already clear about who we are and what we want; it's the mind that gets in the way. And say... my life? I'm living it!

TRY THESE

◻

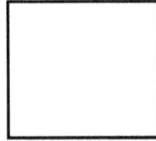

Jason Stephenson meditations
Wim Hof – "control fear by going to it. Not letting it come to you. By challenging our body and mind."
Sacred Acoustics
Books by Henry David Thoreau
Feng Shui
Ho-oPonoPono (forgiveness) prayer
GAIA
Joe Dispenza
Adyashanti
Goop
Techno music means no technology (I think); it's a high-vibrating style of music.
Movies: I Heart Huckabees
The Wrong Missy
Along came Polly
Truman show
Alice in Wonderland
Groundhog Day
Star Wars (may the force be with you)
Elf

Music is the soundtrack to your life

Songs:

Trevor Hall called HOLD ON with Gone gone beyond (so many years just chasing the thoughts in my head)
Imagine Dragons
I'll kill for a drop of your good love
I am blue (lyrics); we are all one
Sia
Elderbrook
Mind Chatter
Crooked Colours
Mome – Moment II (Live session / Los Angeles) ft. Ricky Ducati...
I've been quiet for so long (Marshmallow)
What a feeling (song)
Jack Johnson
Bob Marley
I'm feeling good
One Republic
Labrinth
Mumford and Sons Lyrics say fix my eyes so I can see the lies.
Good Vibes – Binaural Beats

Archetypes
Louise Hay's Emotional Symptoms
The Secret Language of Birthdays
Ground your bed (video on Gaia)
The science of the Mind
Familiar.

I found out that my familiar is the Thunderbird. Its thunder is made from its wings, and lightning shoots out of its third eye. While writing this book,

I shaved the left side of my head and felt it was exposing my truth. The truth is on the left side of your body. The lightning that comes from the Thunderbird's third eye is the truth and its connection to the source.

About me – Jessica Simmonds – jessgoodvibesonly

I am a spiritual being having a human experience as an indigenous woman since 1979 in this reality "lifetime." Currently, I'm a mom of four beautiful souls. I've been a wanderlust for 30 years now.

I have been an entrepreneur (Paramita Academy of Makeup Inc.) and teacher for over two decades. The most enjoyable part of my experience was meeting people and spreading the information I was studying. I am certified in makeup artistry, hypnotherapy, advanced meditation, reiki level two, and neuro-linguistic programming.

I believe in you, so you can believe in yourself!

Please visit: www.aspiritualwarriorspath.com

"Create a life that feels good on the inside, not just one that looks good on the outside."
- UNKNOWN

My Future Wish:

About the author (2022)

Jessica Simmonds is the author of the international bestsellers A Spiritual Warrior's Path series. She is a popular public speaker and travels worldwide to promote her work, and her inspirational way of being has inspired millions.

As my Grammy would always say, GOOD LUCK TO YOU and see you in the movies!

"

OM represents everything (wakefulness, dreaming, and deep sleep. Past, present, future)

"

"

"Life is not going to go your way. You have to go your way and take life with you."

- Jay Shetty

"The world isn't against you or with you. You create your own reality in every moment."

"Life isn't happening to us; it's happening for us."

"

www.ingramcontent.com/pod-product-compliance
Lightning Source LLC
Chambersburg PA
CBHW052130030426
42337CB00028B/5097